Expect to Manifest Your Best Life

Activating the Law of Positive Expectation

By Elena G. Rivers

All rights reserved. No part of this publication may be reproduced, stored in a retrieval system, or transmitted, in any form or by any means, electronic, mechanical, photocopying, recording, or otherwise, without the author and the publishers' prior written permission.

The scanning, uploading, and distributing this book via the Internet or any other means without the author's permission are illegal and punishable by law. Please purchase only authorized electronic editions and do not participate in or encourage electronic piracy of copyrighted materials.

Elena G. Rivers © Copyright 2022 - All rights reserved.

ISBN: 978-1-80095-096-2

Legal Notice:

This book is copyright protected—it is for personal use only.

Disclaimer Notice:

Please note that the information contained in this book is for inspirational and entertainment purposes only. Every attempt has been made to provide accurate, up-to-date, and completely reliable information. No warranties of any kind are expressed or implied. Readers acknowledge that the author is not engaging in the rendering of legal, financial, health, medical, or professional advice. By reading this book, the Reader agrees that under no circumstances are we responsible for any losses, direct or indirect, which are incurred due to the use of the information contained within this book, including, but not limited to, errors, omissions, or inaccuracies. The information provided in this book is for entertainment purposes only. If you are struggling with serious problems, including chronic illness, mental instability, or legal issues, please consult with your local registered health care or legal professional as soon as possible. This book is not a substitute for professional or legal advice.

Contents

Introduction: Expect to Manifest Your Best Life (Because You Can!) 6

Secret #1 The Energy of Positive Expectation... 18

Secret #2 Different Kinds of Wanting and Desiring 34

Secret #3 Planting a Positive Seed of Your Dream Reality 52

Conclusion- You Are a Manifesting Machine! 66

Join Our Manifestation Newsletter and Get a Free eBook 76

Introduction: Expect to Manifest Your Best Life (Because You Can!)

Is it wrong to want something? Can we want something and manifest it into our lives? If you've been studying the Law of Attraction, you may feel a bit confused. After all, some teachers say that you should release the need to want something because when you want something, it means you don't have it...

And some say it's OK to want more and reach higher goals as it fuels your ambition and desire...

A friend who knows I write about the Law of Attraction has recently asked me about my stand on wanting...

He asked: "Elena, so which side do you take?".

My answer was: *both*.

Because both attitudes are correct!

Wanting something or wanting more of what you've already manifested is not bad, so release any need to feel guilty for wanting more.

Introduction – Expect to Manifest

At the same time, some people in certain life situations might benefit from taking the attitude of not wanting anything if they choose to do so. And we can always choose.

Now, let's focus on wanting...You see, it all depends on your energy. For example, you may want something outside of yourself, and when you think about it, you may experience the feelings of "I don't have it yet, I don't feel worthy."

Of course, such an attitude is wanting from a place of lack and it can delay your manifestations.

But don't feel bad if you have caught yourself wanting something and then experienced negative feelings about it. We have all been there. I also experience those feelings sometimes. Yet, my life and manifesting practice keep getting better and better.

How is that so? Am I just lucky? What's my secret?

Well, I have a little secret, something I've been sharing in my recent books, and many of my readers resonated with this concept. It actually gave them a massive relief from fearing negative thoughts!

Introduction – Expect to Manifest

It's simple. I made a decision that ONLY my positive thoughts and states manifest. And this is what I believe, assume, and expect to be true for me. You can also believe, assume and expect that ONLY your positive thoughts and states manifest! And allow it to be so.

So, starting right here, right now, start affirming: "Only my positive thoughts manifest!"

Now, a word of caution…

Is this belief system like a green light to indulge in negativity?

No, of course not. But it's so liberating. We get to save so much time and energy to focus on creating our best selves and our best lives with joy, ease, and confidence.

So, let's release all that fear and superstition. You can't even imagine how many sleepless nights I spent worrying about having negative thoughts. And some of these thoughts were really not that bad. Some just wanted to give me an idea to take better care of myself or my business. For example, to check travel insurance for my upcoming trip or talk to my accountant regarding some invoices. Yet, my undisciplined mind would turn those thoughts into worry. It kept attaching extremely elaborate stories to even a slightly negative thought…

"Oh, if I have this thought, it's probably because something bad will happen on my trip…or I'll get audited… or lose everything. And who knows what!"

I would spend days worrying that now I may manifest some of those thoughts I had…

All those negative thoughts would drain my creative energy, so I couldn't do anything. Since I wasn't very productive or efficient, I wouldn't get any good results and so achieving my goals was very hard.

And then I desperately tried to think about something positive to cancel out my initial negative thoughts (that, by the way, weren't even that negative, it's just that my fear made them more and more negative).

It was so, exhausting! Jumping from one extreme (fear and worry) to the next (trying to be positive). It took me a while to do some self-investigation to discover that the root of all my problems with manifesting was the fear of negative thoughts and the expectancy that they would manifest into something horrible! Oh and I kept on living with constant self-blame and inner critic.

Many of my readers were reporting precisely the same issue. They got into LOA and got scared of thinking negative thoughts.

Well, it's time to release all that simply by deciding that ONLY your positive thoughts manifest and that you are safe and well taken care of by the Universe.

And feeling negative emotions is human and nothing to be ashamed of. There are many healing modalities, such as EFT Tapping (Emotional Freedom Technique), Faster EFT, or the Sedona Method, aimed at helping you process and release negative emotions. I always recommend those modalities to my readers as I think that for many, it may be a missing piece to the Law of Attraction and happy and peaceful living in general.

So, once again, there's nothing to fear. Whenever there's negativity in your mind, you can choose to release it and tell yourself that only your positive thoughts and states manifest.

Introduction – Expect to Manifest

And yes, your job is to focus on positive thoughts as much as possible. Look at what I'm doing in this book…I'm helping you harness the power of positivity. Instead of making you feel bad for having negative thoughts and guilt tripping you that you will manifest something horrible into your life, I'm helping you understand that you get to choose your own expectations and manifesting rules!

Make it your affirmation- *only my positive thoughts manifest*.

Boom. Done! It's as simple as that!

But don't ignore other thoughts, even the more negative ones. Don't be afraid of them either; simply see them as healing messengers because that's what they're for. They appear to provide you with a message that there's some part of you that needs to be transformed.

Some negative thoughts might tell you it's time to embark on a healing journey. When I say "healing," I don't mean dwelling on the past. Healing is about transforming negative into positive. It all starts with awareness. And we can be grateful for our negative

Introduction – Expect to Manifest

thoughts and treat them as powerful reminders to dive deeper.

Some negative thoughts may remind you to be grateful for what you have. Some negative thoughts might be telling you to take better care of yourself.

And some negative thoughts might be intuitive downloads to remind you to take certain precautions such as improving your insurance policy, double-checking your legal obligations, or getting a medical check-up.

Let's not forget that we live in the physical world that is also governed by physical as well as man-made laws.

But once again, improving your health insurance doesn't mean that you're automatically preparing for the worst-case scenario and expect to get sick, which will manifest as some horrible disease. You can check or improve your insurance policy or whatever needs to be taken care of from a powerful state of feeling secure and well taken care of.

As one of my favorite quantum physics teachers, Vadim Zeland puts it beautifully: "Take care without worry!"

Introduction – Expect to Manifest

There are two extremes we want to avoid. One of them is being too attached to this physical plane, worrying too much about all possible negative scenarios, and taking too many preventative measures and actions from a place of lack, scarcity, worry, fear and doubt.

The second extreme is spiritual escapism, where a person refuses to take any physical action. The mindset behind it is: "If I take any action to protect my house from, let's say, being flooded, even though floods are quite common in my area, it means I am preparing for it and will automatically manifest it, so let's not do anything and hope for the best."

Yes, it may work, but you may also lose your home! Of course, the examples I'm sharing are exaggerated, but I hope you understand my point. It's all about bridging the physical with the spiritual. The Universe operates by the Law of Least Resistance, and sometimes it may want you to double-check your insurance policy and be done with it because that's the easiest way to go about things.

I mention all this in the introduction because there are many superstitious misconceptions about the Law of

Introduction – Expect to Manifest

Expectancy. These can make many people, especially those sensitive ones, feel scared, guilty, or negative.

And we practice manifestation to have fun, right?

I can't tell you how much relief I experience by incorporating the belief that "Only my positive thoughts manifest."

And now, even when something crops up and requires fixing, I approach everything from a relaxed and positive mindset. I remind myself of Vadim Zeland's words: "Take care without worry." I do what's required in the given moment and then let go and move on, knowing that I'm well taken care of by the Universe.

I no longer beat myself up that it's all my fault because I probably thought negatively about something a while ago. Whenever I realize I'm thinking about something negative, I simply say: "cancel, cancel." And I visualize a big STOP sign. I also like to add: "I'm only available for peace, love, and positivity. But thank you for bringing this to my awareness because it means more healing for me!"

Introduction – Expect to Manifest

So, I hope this little intro helped clear out some negativity around the Law of Expectation. This is why I included the word: "positive" in the subtitle.

We are here to unleash the power of positive expectations and live a positive life. You're not manifesting anything negative into your life, so release any guilt or doubt. God, Angels, and the Universe equipped you with the most powerful manifesting powers for your highest good. They would never intend for you to manifest something terrible on purpose!

Yes, as Abraham-Esther Hicks share, we came to Earth to experience contrast. We know and understand that sometimes we may face negative situations and circumstances and that we shouldn't blame ourselves or our thoughts for that.

Also, the contrast we may experience is not designed as some punishment from the Universe. However, it may motivate you to consciously improve some areas of your life.

For example, after being diagnosed with an autoimmune condition, I experienced contrast.

Introduction – Expect to Manifest

-"Why me?"- I thought.

But then, I reminded myself that I still had a choice and could use my condition to learn more about self-care and healthy living. So, in my case, the initial contrast I experienced served me as what Esther-Abraham Hicks refer to as "the catapult."

It helped me change my habits and take better care of myself. In fact, it helped me reach new heights of wellness. I also inspired many of my family and friends to change their relationship with self-care.

One of the concepts I applied to my health journey was that of positive expectation. I simply decided that something positive would come out of what seemed to be very negative, and so it did.

Now, as a conscious writer, it is my responsibility to mention that I'm not a medical professional, and I'm not saying that the positive thinking techniques I'm sharing can be used to substitute medical or legal help you may need. However, from my experience, the power of positive expectation can make any professional program or course of action much more effective, whether it's healing, career, business, or improving your relationships!

So, keep repeating that only your positive thoughts manifest...

Only my positive thoughts manifest.

Only my positive thoughts manifest.

Only my positive thoughts manifest.

All other thoughts are valuable messengers to help you transform on a deeper level and face your shadows (but that would be a topic for another day, for now, let's dive fully into the Law of Positive Expectation!)

Secret #1 The Energy of Positive Expectation

To quickly recap what we've explored in the previous chapter – it's all about *the energy* behind expecting something or nothing. Both approaches can serve you, depending on your situation.

For example, many spiritual teachings often refer to, or recommend, the mindset of not wanting and not expecting anything. Or perhaps embarking on a new journey (such as personal transformation, new job, business, learning a new skill) with no expectations.

To say that if a person doesn't expect anything, they will get nothing is a huge misinterpretation of the Law of Expectancy.

What we really need to look into to discover how it works is *the energy* behind the mindset of not wanting or not expecting anything.

For example, a person can decide and declare they don't want or expect anything because they feel defeated. Deep inside, they believe they're not worthy of their desires, or perhaps, they experienced a failure that traumatized them or hurt their confidence.

I have been in such a dark place many times, and it would never work out for me. I just kept attracting more defeat and more insecurities.

Eventually, I had to face my shadows and allow myself to fail so that I could learn. To do so, I studied the biographies of successful and famous people and realized that failure can lead to success. And failure doesn't have to feel bad. It doesn't have to feel like failure!

So, that changed my perspective a lot. Then, I also worked with several energy healers to release my energetic blocks (this is optional, but if you feel called to try energy healing, definitely go for it!). I discovered beautiful self-healing modalities such as Reiki and EFT tapping, which I now practice on myself daily.

Thanks to my experience, I can quickly tell when I'm beginning to feel defeated (and I can shift myself out of such a funky state!). At the same time, whenever I talk to someone who tells me they don't expect anything and don't want anything, I immediately know if they're making such a statement and decision from negative energy of defeat, guilt, anger, and not believing in themselves.

Energy is everything! Just like in the world of business, they say: "numbers never lie" on my manifesting journey, I quickly realized *that energy never lies.*

And I can also feel that you and other readers of this book either already know and understand this truth or are in some process of discovering it. The more you read books like this one or any books aimed at helping you unleash new levels of self-awareness, the more you develop terrific abilities to know what is good for you and what is not. Intuitively!

So, to recap, the first scenario behind not wanting and expecting anything is that a person simply feels defeated and feels like nothing will work for them. They may sign up for a program, hire a coach, or other professional. Still, their prevailing energy of feeling like a failure will not activate the Law of Positive Expectations, so they may find themselves stuck in their old ways.

Secret #1 The Energy of Positive Expectation

My heart goes to everyone feeling so defeated or disappointed because I have been there for many years. But if you're feeling defeated and you're reading this book, it means you still believe there's a way out. There's hope. So, promise yourself to choose a different scenario.

Remember that you are a powerful creator. You're not a failure, and nothing is wrong with you. We all experience our ups and downs. Forgive yourself and turn your failures and mistakes into valuable lessons. If you need more guidance, you may benefit from reading my book: *Self-Love Handbook*.

You can tune into new possibilities and create the amazing life you rightfully deserve. Manifesting is our birthright, and you're a powerful child of the Divine/ God / the Universe- or whatever Higher Power you believe in.

Now, onto the second scenario. A person could also say that they start something with no expectations. For example, they commence on new projects with no expectations, from the positive energy of letting go and

Secret #1 The Energy of Positive Expectation

outsourcing the final results to the Universe/ Higher power.

I have tried this energy and mindset myself many times, and it worked beautifully every time, as long as my energy was pure, and I believed in myself.

For example, I felt inspired to start a mini freelance side hustle at some stage. As I was meditating, something told me to research different freelance websites. And so, I did. I found over twenty of them and offered my services on those websites. As I went into this process, I felt guided all the time. It all felt like an inspired action. Even though many of my applications were rejected, I still found several wonderful clients, and we enjoyed working together. And rejected applications served me as a valuable lesson to improve my communication and positioning skills. So, they were feedback from the Universe that helped me grow.

Then, some potential clients were not the best energetic match for me, or I wasn't the best match for them. But luckily for me, I didn't create any negative stories around the initial rejections I experienced. Deep inside, I knew I was following a path I was guided to follow, and I just knew that something positive would come out of my calling! And yes, the Universe rewarded me with many amazing and generous clients, who, on top of our agreed payments, also felt like offering me bonuses.

When I embark on a new journey, I often like to set goals for myself because I want to see and celebrate my progress through different small steps and milestones. But this time, I felt inspired to outsource the final results to the Universe. You know the saying – let go and let in God?

Well, that is what I felt inspired to do.

My energy was so immersed in the process I created for myself, interacting with different leaders and business owners and then thinking of numerous ways my skills and experience could help them grow.

The process in itself was so much fun, and it enriched me in so many different ways! I'd even go as far as to say that the process I went through seeking freelance work and gigs taught me so much more than many courses I've taken or seminars I attended. As one of my friends who's a brilliant conscious marketer always says: *nothing can beat learning in practice.*

So, promise yourself it will be all right, roll up your sleeves, and keep working behind the scenes.

My little spiritual add-on to this life philosophy is: Outsource the final result to whatever Higher Power you believe in. Be so passionate about your work that there's no room for negativity or doubt.

So, even though I wasn't expecting a super specific result, I was successful with this little side venture because, deep inside, I had a positive feeling and expectation about it.

Once you've truly grasped the energy behind it, it will be so liberating! And again, another person may have a similar idea or goal but create specific outcomes they desire to manifest. There's no right or wrong, as long as your energy is full of positive expectations.

My readers often ask me if I recommend goal setting for manifesting. Specifically, money and income-related goal setting. And, yes, there's a tremendous value in goal setting. If you want to understand the

Secret #1 *The Energy of Positive Expectation*

psychology of goal setting, I'd highly recommend you check out books written by Thibault Meurisse, who is a French personal development author specializing in goal setting.

I learned a lot from him and released many negative mindsets around goal setting. I especially recommend his goal-setting workbook: *The Ultimate Goal Setting Planner: Become an Unstoppable Goal Achiever in 90 Days or Less.* I found it very helpful as I was going through the process of successfully manifesting the creation and launch of my blog.

However, for the purpose of mastering manifestation and energy work, please remember that there's no right or wrong. Your energy never lies. You activate the Law of Positive Expectation if you feel good about your goal and create good energy around it. Now, if setting specific goals and numbers make you feel even better- go for it!

At the same time, if you prefer to go into something with no specific expectations (other than everything will turn out amazingly well for you) and outsource the final results to the Universe, definitely give it a go!

If you choose to do so, embrace this mindset: let me just work on it with my best energies and allow the Universe to surprise me with excellent results!

By the Law of You – <u>you create your own rules</u>.

Rules should not feel like rules. They should not restrict us. If anything, they can empower and guide us. But at the end of the day, it's all up to you!

I think that many readers will benefit from this tip, especially those who felt burned out by traditional goal setting and hustling their way to success. At the same time, it can also help those who perhaps feel confused about goal setting...

I mean, what's the best way? High goals?

Or not-so-high goals so that we can achieve them faster and develop a belief that we can achieve what we want?

Both approaches can work great for manifesting.

Suppose you feel inspired to follow high-goal-setting teachings because high goals make you feel good. You dive deep, and you feel there's no doubt in your mind that you can achieve your desire. You create potent energy of positive expectation. You will stay focused on your goal until you reach it and even beyond it.

As one of my favorite teachers from the Secret, Bob Proctor, put it: "Be like a postage stamp. Stick to it until you get there".

I'll add to it- <u>even when you get there, keep expanding, because you can!</u>

However, if high goal setting doesn't make you feel good and triggers self-doubt or disbelief, I'd recommend you dive into inner work aimed at helping you straighten your self-belief and self-concept. My book: *Self-Image Demystified* might be a great place to start!

You may also benefit from working with an energy healer or mindset coach to help you release the blocks preventing you from shining your best self. At the same time, you may start with smaller goals that feel easier to achieve. Then, by achieving them, you develop more confidence and belief in yourself. The most important thing to remember- is don't allow yourself to stew in your old, negative mindsets and energies!

Secret #1 The Energy of Positive Expectation

Here's a set of my favorite positive affirmations to help you unleash the power of positive expectation:

Everything happens for me.

Every day I'm getting better, wiser, and stronger.

I'm an infinite being with infinite potential.

I am a fast learner, and I love learning new things.

I add value to the world.

I inspire other people.

I am worthy, and I make other people feel worthy.

My goals excite me.

I am very good at manifesting.

I can channel my energy into anything I want.

I am a beautiful child of the Universe.

I forgive myself and others.

I value myself.

I am very good at... (add the skill you're learning or your field of expertise).

Plus, a quick tip and affirmation I learned from Dr. Joseph Murphy. It works great, if you're feeling overwhelmed because you need to master something new. You're just starting out and it feels like so much to take in! This could be learning a new language, mastering a new advertising platform, or getting used to a new workplace.

When it comes to overcoming challenges related to learning new things, Dr. Joseph Murphy recommends this super simple affirmation: "I am going to master you!".

That's it. Seriously!

So, whenever you're learning something new or embarking on a new journey, simply stare it in the eye and say: "I am going to master you!".

Then, keep enhancing your belief with positive affirmations related to what you're mastering. Of course, if you're still in the process of learning something, you don't want to go around and brag to other people about how good you are. We don't want to get delusional. And my personal recommendation is to keep your inner work to yourself. If you want to share your manifesting practice with others, share it with your mentor, spiritual teacher, or a support group/mastermind of people on the same journey. You don't want any nay-sayers to poison your vibration.

While I no longer believe that other people's energies can affect my manifestations (simply because of my new empowering belief that only my positive thoughts manifest), let's be mindful of one thing...

Sharing your inner work with people who are not into manifesting can only lead to many unnecessary questions. Such a situation may make you feel like you have to explain or justify yourself. To me, it's not worth my time and energy. So, I keep my inner work to myself and only share my manifesting process with those who are into manifesting, spirituality and self-development or with people I know I can fully trust.

But hey, that's my way! Perhaps you feel differently about sharing, so always tune into your Higher Self and follow your own way.

Also, be mindful of your self-talk. Be your own cheerleader. Say nice things to yourself to help you manifest with joy and ease, and supercharge your confidence! How you treat yourself is more important than some random manifesting techniques. For example, you could visualize or affirm for hours but still be negative and beat yourself up or diminish your success and achievements for the rest of the day, canceling the positivity of your spiritual practices.

If you want to embrace the power of positive expectation, start auditing your thoughts and your self-talk. Your thoughts always put you in a state of a trance. The question is, is it positive or negative trance?

Whenever you catch yourself in a negative "trance," break it by asking yourself the following questions:

-Is this thought good for my wellbeing? Can I let it go?

-If it seems complicated to let go, can I ask the Higher Power for help and focus on something more positive?

-Can I simply allow myself to think about the things I like? What about happy memories?

-Can I visualize myself doing the things I love just to feel good?

Secret #1 The Energy of Positive Expectation

Then, reclaim the power of positive self-talk and positive expectation by saying:

-I always attract amazing things into my life!

-I am worthy of manifesting my desires!

-I feel grateful for everything I've already manifested into my life!

-I allow myself to be patient and take little baby steps daily.

-Everything always works out for me!

-Only my positive thoughts manifest!

-I love thinking positive thoughts because it feels good and natural

Secret #2 Different Kinds of Wanting and Desiring

For the purpose of this book and chapter, I'm using the words: "want" and "desire" interchangeably. Most Law of Attraction books, especially the classics like *Think and Grow Rich,* stick to the word: "desire." The younger generation of LOA/ manifesting teachers and explorers that share mostly through new social media platforms use the word: "want."

The word "want" is more common in everyday conversations, such as: "I want a cup of coffee." We don't really say: "I desire a cup of coffee," right? That would be weird.

But once again, for the purpose of mastering the art of conscious manifesting, we can use both: "want" and "desire." It doesn't really matter which words we use, but the energy we attach to these words. Languages change all the time. New generations create new words. Even grammar changes.

Secret #2 Different Kinds of Wanting and Desiring

Yes, words are very powerful. Sometimes changing even a few words can re-direct our conversations to something better and help us improve our relationships.

But words are merely an expression of our essence, energy, and feelings. So, instead of getting too fixated on words, let's look at the energy from which these words are spoken or written.

People can want or desire something outside themselves and attach negative feelings of not having their desires. Or perhaps they want or desire something, and instead of taking inspired action towards their goals, they look for excuses. Or maybe they feel envious of other people who are already successful.

Some people want or desire something, or they say they do, but deep inside, they want something else. In other words, they pursue wants, goals, and desires that are not even theirs, to begin with. I have been guilty of such a mindset, and it wasn't the best place to be in!

Well, in this case, wanting or desiring is not good. It would be much more beneficial for such a person to dive into inner work aimed at self-awareness and healing to find their own path. What I found very helpful on my journey of self-discovery was Vadim Zeland's book *Reality Transurfing*.

Firstly, it helped me realize that many of my old wants and desires were not really mine. Instead, I was burning myself out to desperately try to please others and seek approval. That book also taught me a lot about the negative energies of guilt and how to release them. What's even more important, it taught me how to stay away from manipulators and follow my own path without wasting time explaining myself to others. That message resonated with me, and I read Vadim's book several times. Each time I discovered more and more about my true myself.

What happened next is that through my work as an author, I met another author (also called Elena) who writes about narcissistic abuse. I wanted to support her and began reading her books, only to realize how many narcissistic people I had attracted into my life and that, unfortunately, many of my family members and early caretakers were also narcissistic. I felt shocked because, for so many years, I had no clue that I'd been a victim of narcissistic abuse, and I'd felt like something was wrong with me. But on the other hand, I felt liberated because it all started to make sense...

I felt like the Universe made me passionate about the Law of Attraction. Which became my career. Which led me to meet an author who opened my eyes to the detrimental effects of narcissistic abuse.

Why am I mentioning all this in a book about positive expectations? Shouldn't I keep it all positive?

One of the messages I'm very consistent with in all my books is that we are often conditioned to either not know what we want or feel confused. And if you've ever experienced toxic abuse or were a victim of gaslighting, it may take some time to find yourself again. What I had to do was to give myself some time to heal and realign myself moving forward.

Perhaps you don't know what you want or what your purpose is. That's OK. Simply enjoy the journey. At the same time, keep auditing your true motivations. Do you want or desire something because you feel like it's your own goal, or is it something you feel like you should get to gain the approval of others?

Secret #2 Different Kinds of Wanting and Desiring

From my experience, gaining the approval of others never works. The first step in any conscious manifestation process is ensuring that what you want or desire comes from your heart. Remember that the power is within you, and you matter. Everyone has their own unique desire, their own unique code. It's just that sometimes the negative conditioning of our society or abuse you might have suffered takes you away from your own truth. Your mind focuses on survival and not so much on thriving and unleashing your true potential.

So, remember that you absolutely deserve all the time you need to get to know yourself and your authentic desires.

Now, I'm not an expert on narcissistic abuse or gaslighting. If you need more information or help, I highly recommend you check out books written by Elena Miro, a psychologist, and sociologist specializing in narcissistic abuse and gaslighting recovery. And, as I've already suggested (both in this book and my other books), *Reality Transurfing* by Vadim Zeland is a beautiful book if you're on a journey of self-discovery and self-liberation.

Secret #2 Different Kinds of Wanting and Desiring

It takes a unique metaphysical approach but is very practical. Reading both Miss Miro and Mr. Zeland is an excellent combo of modern psychology and science with metaphysics and energetics.

OK, so to recap, we've covered the importance of knowing your goals. I also shared with you some extra tips and resources you can use if you feel lost and don't know what you want, or you suffered trauma or abuse and felt like your dreams were taken away from you, or you didn't receive enough support.

Please note that even if you don't know your true goals, you can still study and practice manifestation!

Because manifesting doesn't have to be only about reaching your big goals or desires related to your unique life path or life purpose. Manifesting small things such as feeling energized throughout the day, meeting new people, feeling productive and creative, and attracting new opportunities is not only fun but it can also strengthen your belief and help you on your journey to discovering your purpose.

In fact, these small positive actions, taken from a place of positive expectation, can create real miracles in your life.

Make this your little mantra:

"I do the best I can with what I know, and everything I do helps me reach my full potential. My life keeps getting better and better every day. I'm manifesting a happy, healthy, and abundant life. "

Don't compare yourself to others. Just be yourself and follow your small action steps, things that enrich you and make you feel good, all with positive expectations that something good will come out of it, and it will be so.

I now approach many projects or educational programs I invest in to learn new things from such a mindset. It's liberating and helps me create better results while enjoying the process. Instead of worrying about the final outcome, I simply allow myself to do the best I can every day and love myself, even if I make a mistake.

Secret #2 Different Kinds of Wanting and Desiring

As my partner always says, if you make a mistake and learn from it, it's no longer a mistake! So, why keep poisoning our vibration with self-imposed guilt trips?

OK, so now, let's look at the second scenario.

A person knows what they want or desire. It's their own goal. Will it automatically unleash the power of positive expectation and help them with their past of conscious manifesting?

To answer this question, we need to dive deeper and provide some examples. But first, here's a little back story of how this knowledge came to me…

Several years ago, as I was diligently studying *Think and Grow Rich* by Napoleon Hill and *Reality Transurfing* by Vadim Zeland. At first, I felt very confused!

It seemed to me that Mr. Hill was all for having big desires (and so were many other LOA books). But at the same time, one of my favorite authors who helped me so much on my self-discovery journey, Mr. Zeland, clearly stated that desiring something too much and putting it on a pedestal may even turn against you…

Secret #2 Different Kinds of Wanting and Desiring

It took me a while to figure it out. And as always, both approaches can be correct. We need to dive deeper and take a look at our energy.

I understand that what Mr. Zeland really means is that desire charged with negative, needy energy that is not backed up with any positive action or belief is not good for us.

An example from my own life: in the past, I'd often come up with a goal and desire, and then the first thing I'd do was brag to everyone about it!

Some of the people I would share my ambitious goals with would just laugh at me, and I would be left very discouraged. Now, I no longer blame them because I have come to acknowledge that my old behaviors might have been a bit annoying for some people. Don't get me wrong, I am not saying it's OK to laugh at someone or ridicule them just because they are annoying. But how I'd communicate my goals and desires might have felt like bragging, haha!

Readers of one of my previous books, *Speak to Manifest,* know my story and how I transformed from

Secret #2 Different Kinds of Wanting and Desiring

someone who talked a lot but did very little to a peaceful and effective self-leader.

By saying "a peaceful self-leader," I'm referring to someone who has a positive self-image and operates from calm confidence.

They take meaningful and inspired action while always making progress and celebrating it. They don't waste their energy on mindless talking. Instead, they use all their precious energy to embody their desires to get better every day.

I like to call it Gradual Manifesting, which is a whole new topic, and I may even write a book about it at some point. So many people desire to manifest quantum leaps and feel discouraged if it doesn't work. Let me share my perspective- Gradual Manifesting feels much more magical!

Because every day of your life gets better and better. And as it gets better and better, your past also gets better, and you automatically heal it, and because of the healed past, everything keeps improving. So, this is the power of consistent, positive actions!

Gradual Manifesting eventually leads to Quantum leaps because you choose to embody your best self every day.

Now, back to my old self and what I've learned since then.... Another thing that would very often happen is that I'd brag about my ambitious plans, goals, and desires and was lucky enough to encounter people who were kind, loving, and compassionate. Well, what would you do as a kind person? You'd probably share some words of encouragement, right? And that's what they would do. They would praise and encourage me.

But it didn't work for me either. Do you know why? Because my brain would take these words as complements. I would get nice dopamine hits. I would think: "OK, I got some appreciation for my ambitious goals! It feels like now I'm done."

And because of that, I would never move forward. Instead, I would quit. I often felt such a massive gap between the kind words of compliments I'd receive from others, people who'd express their admiration for my ideas, and my actual self-worth, mindset, and skill set that I just felt hopeless. So, in the end, I would always quit (even before trying...).

It felt like constant struggle. I would allow my ego to stew me in my ambitious goals and desires until I would lose any creative ability to turn my dreams into reality.

This is my understanding and personal experience of something Vadim Zeland calls "creating an excess potential." And I used to be the Queen of Excess Potential!

After all, action is a part of attraction...

For example, if you want to become a high-level professional, entrepreneur, artist, creative, healer, athlete, etc., you need aligned actions to get new skills and develop your abilities.

As a light worker turned writer, I take daily actions to write my books, articles, and newsletters. I also take daily actions to practice my favorite energy healing modalities to stay inspired and gain new insights I can share with my readers. I don't just talk about writing or

Secret #2 Different Kinds of Wanting and Desiring

doing inner work. I simply do it and so every day, I manifest my best life.

But my actions feel good to me and don't burn me out. I'm not hustling or trying hard to get something from someone. I just show up and do my own thing. I'm hired by the Universe, and I follow its orders.

At the same time, many manifestations don't require physical activity. They happen on autopilot as a positive side-effect of you feeling good, embodying your best self, staying grateful for your life, and being mindful of your energies. Positivity always pays enormous dividends. So, even if you don't have any specific goals or don't know what you want, you can feel empowered knowing that creating a positive lifestyle can be a goal in itself!

What needs to be avoided is creating contradicting energies and massive discrepancies between your desires and current state or putting your desires on a pedestal. Vadim Zeland refers to such energetic conditions as creating excess potential.

And as I shared several pages ago, I used to be very good at it. If you'd known me back then, you'd probably have called me the Leading Expert in Creating Excess Potential! I'd always put my desires on a pedestal and kept separating myself from them. I wasn't mindful of my thoughts, actions, energetic states, or how I talked to myself and others. And as you already know, many of my so-called goals weren't even mine, to begin with.

But luckily, Vadim's book, which, as I already told you, I diligently studied and read several times, opened my eyes to what happens if we desire something too much but don't back it up with calm confidence and mindful action.

Because the truth is that back then, I didn't believe in myself. So, I needed external validation. That would lead me to share my ambitious ideas, plans, and goals with others. And no matter what they said, I always felt very discouraged.

But you see, this is where the art of manifesting comes in. To me, manifesting is something we do with our minds and hearts to become whoever we need to be to manifest whatever we desire. So, if you really want something, simply take a few deep breaths and promise yourself to be calm.

Secret #2 Different Kinds of Wanting and Desiring

Mindfully roll up your sleeves and allow yourself to be behind the scenes. Immerse yourself in inner work to expand your mindset and shift your vibrational energy to be aligned with your goals and desires (my previous book, *Manifesting Alignment,* might be of help if you need to dive deeper).

When you reach a state of belief, proceed to whatever steps you are guided to do in alignment with your goals. There's no need to explain anything to anyone. Talking too much about your desires can be very detrimental to your energy. Wouldn't it be better to use your creative energies to manifest your heart's desires and live a happy life?

Of course, having a support system can be very helpful. So, if you need to share your goals, choose a person you can trust or find a mentor or teacher who can guide you. You can also start your own mastermind or support group and create a safe, peaceful environment to facilitate the energy of growth, expansion, and support.

Secret #2 Different Kinds of Wanting and Desiring

In other words, be mindful about what you share, how you share it, and with whom. Trust me, it will help you save time, energy, and resources!

You are under no obligation to share everything with everyone.

Also, remember that staying too focused on your desires and doing so from a place of longing, desperation, neediness, and not having creates negative energy, something Mr. Zeland refers to as excess potential. It's hard to create the energy of positive expectation if you're in such a mindset, right?

You need to be in an absolute alignment where your thoughts, beliefs, feelings, and actions correspond to that which you desire. You're on the same vibration. Then, it's a pure desire, something Mr. Zeland refers to as *the unity of heart and mind*, and Mr. Hill refers to as *a burning desire*.

Now, personally, I don't like the word "burning" because it reminds me of stewing myself in my own desires (and getting burned!).

But once again, words are just words. What really matters is the energy behind them.

What I believe Mr. Hill meant was pure desire. A desire that empowers, inspires, and motivates you to reach new heights. A desire that energizes you and makes you feel passionate about your life. A desire that makes you feel good, and it's all about feeling good, right? That's one of the fundamental pillars of joyful and effortless manifesting.

Even when we put in work and effort, it doesn't feel like hard work...

For example, now that I'm one with my biggest desires, empowering people on their manifesting journeys through my writing, I never feel tired or burned out.

Yes, occasionally, I may feel less inspired, and it's usually an indication to have a little break or perhaps immerse myself in other tasks or gigs. However, the most important thing is that today I am better than I was yesterday. This is what I like to call Gradual Manifesting, and it feels so good because you feel free from wanting and needing (from negative energy).

Secret #2 Different Kinds of Wanting and Desiring

You liberate yourself from the pain of past mistakes and what should or could have gone better. You are no longer afraid of "will it ever work for me?". Instead, you feel inspired to take little baby steps each day and do so with love and positive expectation. Every day is filled with beautiful mini manifestations that keep compounding.

When you expect the best- you plant it in your subconscious mind and fuse yourself with it.

Expecting something is like planting a seed and taking care of it in alignment with natural laws.

In the next chapter, we will discuss the best states to be in, to plant whatever seed you desire, the seed of your dream reality!

Secret #3 Planting a Positive Seed of Your Dream Reality

The seed of positive expectation can't be planted anywhere. It needs good soil, and it needs to be well-taken care of. That's the gist of conscious manifesting. So, how do you make sure you create good conditions for your seed?

Well, you need to reach a calm, relaxed state!

You can choose to practice whatever relaxation technique you want. In fact, I'd encourage you to test different relaxation techniques and choose the one you truly enjoy. For me, it's meditation or EFT tapping, or both. Sometimes, I need to take a few deep breaths, become conscious of my body, and relax my muscles. In fact, this is what I very often do on my writing breaks. I simply relax. If I feel any tension in my body, I direct my breathing to it.

You really don't need anything fancy to relax. You just need to start scheduling some mini relaxation breaks. As Nike's slogan says: "Just do it!". Here's what I like to add to motivate you: do it before your mind starts wondering if you're doing it right or if you know enough to get started…!

If you're new to it, start with just one little relaxation ritual a day and take it from there. But trust me, when you experience the blessings of regular relaxation and its importance for manifesting, you'll wonder how you could ever live without it.

All you need to do is give yourself some You Time to relax. Prepare the soil!

If you're still feeling confused or not too sure how to start, the simplest way to go about it is:

Set your timer for 5-10 minutes and turn off your phone. Eliminate distractions. If you want to, you can use some relaxation music, incense sticks, crystals, lavender essential oil, or a relaxing herbal tea. But these are all add-ons! Yes, they may enhance your relaxation experience, but they are not obligatory. A simple meditation done with a strong intention to relax, release and let go is enough!

As you go deep into relaxation, remember that you don't have to do anything. You don't have to think about your desires or how they will come to you. All you need to do now is relax and prepare the soil.

Focus on your breathing. As you breathe in, visualize a beautiful white healing light. As you breathe out, have the intention to release everything that no longer serves you.

Become fully aware of your beautiful body and its unique systems. How does your body work? Everything happens automatically because your body's inner intelligence takes care of everything.

As you go deeper into relaxation and breathing, embrace the beautiful sensations of peace, joy, love, and bliss.

That's it. All you need to do is to relax. By spending more time in relaxation, your thoughts and expectations will become more and more positive, and you'll find yourself attracting more and more positivity.

This is one of the simplest, purest, and most beautiful truths of the Law of Attraction.

So, what's the most important thing you can take away from this book to enhance your manifesting journey?

Secret #3 Planting a Positive Seed

It's simple... Embrace the gift of relaxation. But don't take my word for it...test it yourself! I'm already excited for my readers because I know that the daily gift of relaxation will improve their lives tremendously!

I'll also add this...most of your inner work to embrace the power of positive expectation should be aimed at relaxing. Do it at least once a day.

I don't want to impose any rules on you. You know rules such as what you need to do and how long you should stay in this relaxed state. I don't know you or your schedule. But I intuitively know many of my readers' questions even before I finish my books or submit them for publishing, haha!

And I know that curious and ambitious minds and souls have questions!

But please don't worry about any rules. Simply embrace the gift of daily relaxation in a way that best fits your lifestyle. If you begin to start feeling stressed out about "doing it wrong" or try hard to force yourself into rituals that don't feel good or feel too long, take it as a sign from your Higher Self that you need to slow down and...send your mind on a little break.

Instead, focus on your heart. In fact, as you do your daily relaxation ritual, I'd recommend you focus on your heart as well. In your heart, you're safe. There's no ego. No limitations. No negative "what if's." You can bathe in the pure joys of your heart, knowing that it transports you to a magical quantum field of all possibilities.

That should give your mind some peace! You are relaxing your nervous system while embracing a truly spiritual manifesting ritual.

Now, if you know what your desire is after you've relaxed, you can journal about it using the following (or similar) format:

"I'm so happy and grateful that I manifested (add your desire here)."

For example: "I'm so happy and grateful I manifested my dream job. I love what I do, work with great people, and get paid very well!".

You can also visualize it or affirm it.

That's how you plant a seed. You prepare the soil by relaxing! Yes, that's all there is to it. You relax and soothe your inner state. Then, you plant your seed by using any manifesting technique you may have chosen to follow and take care of it by...

Yes, you guessed. You can take care of it by taking care of your inner state and positive expectation. In other words, becoming conscious of your awareness and how you feel. And by telling yourself that *only* your positive thoughts manifest.

An interesting analogy comes to my mind, and I feel inspired to share it. I first thought about it while writing one of the blog articles and compared manifesting techniques (such as affirmations, visualizations, or scripting) to a bridge that takes you to your new, desired reality.

I'm not the only one using this comparison, as other writers and teachers often use it too. Ultimately, we're all connected and often manifest similar ideas.

But the question that came to my mind several paragraphs ago was: even with this beautiful analogy, why do so many people still feel like they fail with LOA or can't manifest their desires?

Then it dawned on me. The following comparison fits beautifully into this chapter and the importance of relaxation.

Let's say our bridge is located at point #1. And it takes you to point #2.

If you are aware enough, you'll see that there's always a bridge you can mold in any way you desire so that it takes you to #2, your new, desired reality.

But most people never make it to the bridge. Or they desperately try to make it, but when they reach it, the bridge is closed.

Because to make it to the bridge and start walking on it with peaceful confidence while cherishing the view of your desired reality and the process that leads you to it, we need to arrive at point #1 from point #0.

So, what is point #0?

Point #0 is a relaxed, peaceful state that prepares our hearts, minds, and bodies for the journey from point #1 to point #2 while enjoying whatever bridge we create for ourselves.

Secret #3 Planting a Positive Seed

Often, we refuse to enjoy the process and delay our manifestations because we try to jump out of the bridge or get some kind of a shortcut...

But all we need to do to embrace the power of positive expectation is to:

-embrace the gift of daily relaxation where we automatically release what no longer serves us and connect to the magic realm of quantum possibilities

-show up on our mindfully created beautiful bridges with huge smiles on our faces while peacefully and confidently placing one foot in front of the other.

I'll share Vadim Zeland's wise words once again:

"Take care without worry!".

This is how you create your own beautiful bridge and enjoy the journey of gradual manifesting! The following words of empowerment will help you release the shackles of negativity (often self-imposed) and embrace your true power!

Release worry and fear. Why would you worry if your dream reality is so close that it's already brightened up your current reality? When you're happy and grateful for what you already have, the rest is much easier and your journey much more enjoyable.

You can design your life, all aspects of it!

You're not limited by what's happening now or by your past results.

The power of creation available to you is not limited by your past mistakes (that, by the way, are valuable lessons!). If you can visualize it and affirm it or write about it, you can achieve it.

The more you relax and bathe in your heart's worry-free, joyful states, the more you realize your true, infinite potential. Your dream reality is already yours. You can see it. So, don't turn around because your past limitations don't matter unless you want them to matter. The choice is always yours.

As you relax, you realize how powerful you are. Your life is a blank page, and you can write anything you desire. It's your life and your creation!

As you relax, you can fully experience the power of letting go and love-based awareness…

At the same time, remember that you're never alone.

Secret #3 Planting a Positive Seed

The creative power does it with you and through you. You co-create with something bigger...

The Spirit flows through you and expresses yourself as you. What's your form of self-expression?

What's stopping you from expressing yourself fully so you can attract people with the same vibration?

Stop hiding your true light and true potential.

The saying: "Shine so brightly that your haters are gonna need sunglasses," comes to my mind.

But why even expect to have haters?

Why not use your potential to transform hate into love?

Hurt people hurt people. Nobody is born a hater. People turn to hate because nobody taught them how to turn to love.

But by being and embodying love, choosing to be your true self, and walking confidently on your own bridge, you will inspire others to do the same, in their own way.

There's no hate, jealousy, and competition in the new, love-based reality we're building collectively.

We don't manifest success to make others feel jealous or bad. We manifest and fulfill our true, heart-based desires to inspire them so that their souls can awaken to what's possible for them.

It's time to feel safe and create safety for our communities, cities, and the world!

Do not let your current reality or environment limit you. Use your imagination. Go deep within yourself. Live in your heart where all the possibilities exist.

You can create the right environment that empowers you and creates an expectation beyond your wildest dreams. As you do so, you transform your frequency and vibration to inspire others while spreading peace and harmony. Even if you don't say or do anything! That's the power of living in alignment with your authentic energy and using it for the highest good of everyone around you.

You can grow into anything you choose just by changing your expectations…

And once again, it's how you treat yourself. Why not treat yourself to a daily mini resort of relaxation and letting go?

Self-discipline is so much fun. Many people fear the word "discipline" because it leads to deeply ingrained beliefs that we have to discipline ourselves to do something we don't even like to achieve something to impress others and be successful on someone else's terms.

Why not use the gift of mindful self-discipline to transform our mindset and energy to manifest our heart's desires?

This process is simple, enjoyable, stress-free, and fun.

We just need to let go of all the negative conditioning from the past, such as:

"Who has the time to relax?"

"Relaxation is for weak people."

"Gotta keep hustling and pushing."

"Instead of wasting time on some meditations, why not work more?"

Secret #3 Planting a Positive Seed

Let's not forget the saying: "Energy never lies!".

Actions taken from bad energy hardly ever lead to the good results we desire...

So, promise yourself to grow on your own terms. Design your own beautiful garden, the garden of your mind, heart, and soul that is sacred to you.

The Universe wants you to succeed on your terms. Your desires were placed in your heart so you can express them and manifest them fully. As you continue to do so, more and more magical opportunities will start unfolding.

There's no place for fear on your bridge. If your bridge is filled with fear, it's probably not even your bridge, to begin with.

But you can always get back to point "zero," relax, realign and get back on your own bridge. The one that is filled with faith and quiet confidence.

You have nothing to fear. Only your positive thoughts manifest, and you create your own rules.

Secret #3 Planting a Positive Seed

Your system is created to focus on the positive, visualize what you desire, and be in harmonious vibration.

But at some point, you were deceived by people who didn't know this Universal truth and lived by fear-based principles...

Luckily, you can change the channel. You can tune into whatever you want. You own the TV and radio of your life. The most important voice is always the positive and empowering voice of your Higher Self, that magical part of You that loves you unconditionally, takes care of you, and wants nothing but the best for you.

Keep going and enjoy the process. Appreciate the prosperity in all areas of your life because prosperity is your birthright!

Conclusion- You Are a Manifesting Machine!

This final chapter is designed to remind you of the importance of relaxing and building positive expectations in your mind and heart!

You now know you have the power to build an image of your desire, illuminate it with positive expectations, and keep taking positive, aligned action from a place of confidence.

You also know how to let go, so you no longer feel addicted to worry or hopelessness. Fill your mind, day, and actions with positivity. Breathe in positivity as you do your daily relaxation practice.

Remember the quote: "Let go and let in God." A Higher Power is willing to help you. The more you relax and fuse yourself with the creative power of your heart, the more it will reveal itself to you. You can call this power the God, the Divine, Your Guardian Angels or Spirits, the Infinite Intelligence, the Quantum Field, or Your Higher Self. Whatever works for you!

But know that you're never alone and that power is within you.

You activate it through daily relaxation, surrendering to positivity, gratitude, and magic.

Your positive inner states and feelings create positive expectations. So, be mindful of how you feel.

Remember that you can change your internal state whenever you want. All you need to do is to practice the mini-meditations and relaxation techniques I suggested in the last chapter. The more you do them, the better you will feel. The better you feel, the more you attract!

Practice entering relaxed states every day. The Law of Attraction and Expectation reply to repetition and consistency. But of course, everything you do and your inner work activities should feel good.

So, you don't have to go into super long meditations if they're not your thing. Simply infuse your inner work with your unique energy, lifestyle, desires, and personality.

I gave you my own simple process to have something to follow, but my deep desire is that this book will inspire you to practice and do everything your way. The end goal is to feel good and expect good.

Finally, do not allow the society-imposed negativity to steer you away from manifesting the life you rightfully deserve.

The word "discipline" is related to the word "disciple."

It's all about learning, growing, forgiving yourself, and moving forward. It's not about being perfect. It's about progress.

You are a disciple of faith, the Law of Attraction, and expectation. And so, you understand the importance of daily aligned discipline. Small steps repeated daily lead to massive transformations and extraordinary manifestations.

In fact, I'd even go as far as to say that quantum leaps are created by those small baby steps repeated daily (all from a place of feeling good and expecting the best!).

The Law of Expectancy is a very simple law to apply. You don't need any complicated rituals or detailed metaphysical knowledge. Simply follow through with what you've learned in this book. I'd also encourage you to read it more than once because you will find something new that will take your manifesting to the next level each time. Keep reminding yourself that it's all about soothing your inner state. You can manifest so much faster by letting go of fear, worry, stress, and doubt!

At the same time, remember that you are unique! And so is your path.

In fact, you can create your own way of manifesting with it, which, as I've stressed multiple times across all of my books, is one of my biggest desires for my beautiful readers.

I want you to feel free, inspired, empowered, creative, and energized so you can manifest your best life, vibrate high, and inspire others just by being You.

Inspiration means being in Spirit and being connected to the Spirit. I genuinely hope that my work can provide you with inspiration and empowerment to help you re-connect to your own unique power, straight from the Source, straight from the Spirit.

So, rather than being a teacher, I see myself as a messenger. We're all connected!

This little book served as a tool, or our little hang out over a nice cup of coffee or tea, to help you activate the power of positive expectation.

You were born with that extraordinary power of creative light. And even if the past circumstances of your life made you feel defeated, please know that you're never alone. Many of us also felt defeated in one way or another. The most important thing to focus on is transforming whatever unfavorable circumstances you encounter into something positive that can help you and those around you. You are strong enough to embark on this beautiful journey, and I'm excited to hear about your manifesting success story!

Because everything happens FOR you. You manifested this book for a reason. I felt inspired to write it during my daily relaxation meditation. I couldn't focus on anything else until it was finished. Seriously! It felt like the Spirit shared different reader avatars, stories, and personalities I intuitively felt like connecting to and helping through my writing. I also feel like this experience enhanced my empathic ability, and I'm very grateful to you, the Reader, for being a part of this experience.

After all, it's a collective experience of all of us having this magical and revitalizing cup of coffee together. It feels good. It feels natural. It feels fun. That's what manifesting should feel like. That's our natural default manifesting state that we are activating and then enhancing to reach new levels of joy, love, happiness, and all the good stuff life has to offer.

Because The Law of Expectancy is one of the most natural laws, and the truth is we're always expecting something...so why not expect something good, something amazing?

What's stopping you? Some past rejections, fears, or situations? Your point of attraction is now.

Now you know yourself better and are more aware, so it has to work!

Replace the fear of losing something with the pleasure of receiving something amazing.

Failure can be reframed to:" Oh, it's just a stepping stone to manifesting more success."

Instead of beating yourself up with "Oh, I'm such a loser," you can say: "Thank God, I learned my lesson now. I will do better next time!".

You can manifest whatever you desire by choosing to control your reactions and soothe your inner states.

In fact, make it your affirmation:

"I am a manifesting machine."

You expect the best and prepare for the best. So, prepare for the shiny or sunny day. I even named my savings bank account *Sunny Day Account*! And a friend of mine called hers: *Let's Grow*. There are different ways to go about it, as long as you use words that make you feel good and evoke positive images in your mind. To me, *A Sunny Day Account* stands for magical experiences, freedom, and all the fun stuff you can do with money.

My friend likes her way of going about things because she loves the idea of using money to make more money. She loves words such as *growth* or *expansion*.

And it's always interesting to see a reaction you get from your bank's clerk or accountant when they see how creative you are with naming your accounts!

Use your mind to think about the things you love. In fact, make a list of all of them. And then visualize them, just to feel good!

When you reach peaceful and relaxed states, you regain energy and zest for life. Then, you simply expect the best, no matter what you do or what happens in your life. And so, everything gets better. Your wellbeing, your relationships, and your ability to do your job in the most efficient way possible. The way the Universe likes it – well done and through least resistance!

So, use your valuable energy to think about the things you love and re-affirm your gratitude so that your beautiful subconscious mind aligns with your new positive expectations!

Look for health, wealth, and happiness. Instead of reading or watching mainstream news filled with endless negative stories, fill your mind with positive, inspirational videos, podcasts, books, and articles.

Celebrate other people's health, wealth, success, and happiness.

Why not expect your energy levels to get better? And why not create beautiful, delicious, and nourishing meals with this expectation?

Why not expect a salary raise? And why not walk around your office with this calm confidence of being a high earner?

Whatever you think or do can be infused with the energy of positive expectation.

Once again, Dear Reader, I think my work here is done (as far as this book goes). But please know we're connected and on this beautiful journey together!

I always pray for you and your success, happiness, and wellbeing!

Until we meet again (in my other books, if you feel inspired to check them out), I wish you all the best on your manifesting journey.

On the next page, I share some free complimentary resources and free access to my LOA newsletter.

So, if you'd like to stay in touch with me and receive positive messages and notifications about my new book releases and articles, as well as other resources to inspire you I invite you to sign up at no cost. I live and breathe this stuff and love sharing my discoveries with others!

Once again, thank you for taking an interest in my book and reading it to the very last page,

I hope we meet again,

Sending you an abundance of love,

Elena

Your friend and guide in conscious manifesting

Join Our Manifestation Newsletter and Get a Free eBook

To help you amplify what you've learned in this book, I'd like to offer you a free copy of my LOA Workbook – a powerful, 5-day program (eBook & audio) designed to help you raise your vibration while eliminating resistance and negativity.

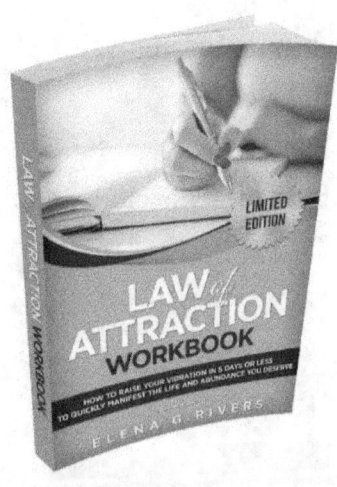

To sign up for free, visit the link below now:

www.loaforsuccess.com/newsletter

More from Elena

You'll also get free access to my inspirational LOA Newsletter to help you stay high vibe!

Through this email newsletter, I regularly share all you need to know about the manifestation mindset and energy.

Plus, whenever I release a new book, you can get it at a deeply discounted price.

To sign up for free, visit the link below or scan the code.

www.loaforsuccess.com/newsletter

If you happen to have any technical issues with your sign-up, please email us at:

support@LOAforSuccess.com

More from Elena

More by Elena G. Rivers:

369 Manifesting Guided Journal

Now available on Amazon:

More from Elena

Manifesting Alignment: Secrets to Becoming a Vibrational Match to Your Desires

More from Elena

Manifestation Meditation: It's Time to Meditate to Attract Your Best Life (Because You Can!)